Soldiers' Sonnet

A Collection of Poems

Sanjay Kumar

notionpress
.com

INDIA · SINGAPORE · MALAYSIA

Copyright © Sanjay Kumar 2024
All Rights Reserved.

ISBN 979-8-89673-075-0

This book has been published with all efforts taken to make the material error-free after the consent of the author. However, the author and the publisher do not assume and hereby disclaim any liability to any party for any loss, damage, or disruption caused by errors or omissions, whether such errors or omissions result from negligence, accident, or any other cause.

While every effort has been made to avoid any mistake or omission, this publication is being sold on the condition and understanding that neither the author nor the publishers or printers would be liable in any manner to any person by reason of any mistake or omission in this publication or for any action taken or omitted to be taken or advice rendered or accepted on the basis of this work. For any defect in printing or binding the publishers will be liable only to replace the defective copy by another copy of this work then available.

Contents

Preface

The journey from the disciplined ranks of the Indian Air Force to the contemplative halls of academia has been both transformative and deeply enriching. In my years of service, I witnessed firsthand the profound sacrifices, unwavering dedication, and silent resilience that define the life of a soldier. These experiences etched deeply into my soul, have now found expression in *Soldiers' Sonnet*.

This collection of poems is a tribute to the indomitable spirit of those who serve and the myriad emotions that accompany them on their journey. From the thrill of duty to the heartache of separation, from the camaraderie of comrades to the silent hope of loved ones left behind, each sonnet captures a facet of the soldier's life. The rhythmic cadence of iambic pentameter, a form chosen deliberately, mirrors the disciplined march of military life, while the rich,

evocative language seeks to convey the depth of emotions that often remain unspoken.

Soldiers' Sonnet is not just a poetic reflection on the life of a soldier; it is also an exploration of the enduring connection between a warrior and their nation, a bond that transcends time, place, and circumstance. It is my hope that these poems resonate not only with those who have worn the uniform but also with readers who wish to glimpse the world through the eyes of those who defend our freedom.

As I transition from the battlefield to the classroom, my goal remains the same: to serve, to inspire, and to share the lessons learned through my journey. This book is an offering to all who value the virtues of duty, honor, and sacrifice. May it stir in you the same passion for service that has guided my life, both in the skies and beyond.

A Mother's Vigil

Upon the hearth, an old and withered hand,
Doth tend the fire that flickers in the night,
Her soldier son now fights in distant land,
While she keeps watch until the morning light.

Her wrinkled face, a map of years long past,
Each line a story of her love and care,
The memories of youth forever cast,
In shadows deep, she offers up a prayer.

She dreams of him, the boy she once did hold,
With tender arms, now worn by time's cruel touch,
Yet in her heart, a strength that won't grow cold,
For though he's gone, she loves him just as much.

The soldier fights, but knows his home is near,
In mother's heart, where he will find no fear.

A Soldier's Matriarch

A matriarch, her heart with sorrow fraught,
For her soldier grandson, far away.
Her eyes, once bright, now clouded,
grief-besought, As days turn into years, a weary fray.

She prays for his return, a fervent plea,
A grandma's love, a beacon in the night.
Her heart, a fragile shell, worn and weary,
As doubts assail, and fill her soul with fright.

A soldier's matriarch, her life forever changed,
By war's harsh grip, that holds her son so tight.
Her hopes and dreams, now scattered, disarranged,
As she awaits, his love, a guiding light.

A grandma's longing, a poignant, mournful plea,
For her soldier grandson, to set her spirit free.

Lament of a Soldier's Bride

With tender vows still fresh upon her lips,
The soldier bids farewell, a duty calls.
Her heart, encased in grief, in silence grips,
As love's first bloom confronts cold duty's walls.

The bridal chamber, warm with dreams just sown,
Now feels the chill of separation's breath.
In every whispered word, a mournful tone,
As fate decrees this bittersweet bequest.

His hand, though strong, shakes softly as they part,
Her eyes, a sea of unshed, glistening tears.
Yet in his gaze, resolve outshines his heart,
Though in its depths, the ache of love appears.

She watches as he fades into the night,
A soldier bound, yet tethered to her light.

Dedication of A Soldier's Wife

With steadfast heart, she waits through endless days,
Her vigil kept, though nights grow cold and long.
In solitude, she walks life's winding maze,
Yet in her soul, her love remains so strong.

Her hands, though soft, have weathered many storms,
As duty's call has taken him afar.
She bears the weight of absence in all forms,
But never does she let it mar her star.

Her every breath, a silent vow she keeps,
To stand beside him, though the miles divide.
In waking hours or in her dream-filled sleeps,
She holds his honour with unyielding pride.

For in her heart, no doubt or fear finds space,
Her love endures, transcending time and place.

Sanjay Kumar

A Soldier's Wife

Awaiting his return, her heart does ache,
 A soldier's wife, alone in empty halls.
 Her eyes, once bright, now filled with shadows black,
 As time's relentless passage slowly crawls.

Each day a year, her hopes begin to fade,
As letters grow scarce, and fears increase.
A lonely heart, a soul that feels betrayed,
 By war's cruel hand, a bitter, cold release.

She dreams of nights spent in his loving arms,
Of laughter shared, of whispered words of love.
But now, she's haunted by war's chilling charms,
 And fears the day his spirit may be lost.

A soldier's wife, her heart forever torn,
 Awaiting his return, a hope forlorn.

A Soldier's Love

A soldier's heart, a love both deep and true,
 For one he leaves behind, a distant dream.
 His eyes, once bright, now filled with sorrow's hue,
As miles divide, and years begin to gleam.

He writes to her, his love, a constant plea,
 A soldier's vow, across the vast expanse.
 Her letters, too, a beacon, wild and free,
A guiding star, that lights his heart's expanse.

A soldier's love, a bond that cannot break,
Through distance, time, and war's relentless might.
 His heart, forever loyal, for her sake,
A steadfast love, a shining, guiding light.

A soldier's love, a testament to grace,
A bond that time and distance cannot erase.

Sanjay Kumar

A Soldier's Daughter

A daughter waits, her heart with longing filled,
For her father's return, a distant dream.
Her eyes, once bright, with sadness now are stilled,
As years pass slowly, like a fleeting stream.

She draws his picture, a faded image, dear,
A memory held close, a precious art.
Her voice, once filled with laughter, now with fear,
As doubts creep in, and tear her heart apart.

A father's absence, a heavy weight to bear,
A child's lone journey, through a world unknown.
Her hopes and dreams, now scattered, lost in air,
As she awaits, her father's love, alone.

A daughter's longing, a poignant, mournful plea,
For her father's return, to set her spirit free.

A Soldier in Forest

Within the verdant gloom of ancient trees,
The soldier treads where shadows weave their snare,
The forest hums with whispers on the breeze,
A primal call that fills the midnight air.

Through tangled roots and underbrush he wades,
His footsteps silent as the owl's flight,
While moonlight filters through the leafy glades,
A ghostly guide amidst the shrouded night.

The canopy, a vaulted, darkened dome,
Enfolds him in its ever-watchful grasp,
Yet undeterred, he claims this wild as home,
With iron will, he tightens duty's clasp.

In forest's depths, where secrets darkly brew,
The soldier stands, both fierce and ever true.

Sanjay Kumar

A Soldier's Billet

In humble billet, far from fields of war,
The soldier rests, where peace is seldom found.
His weary bones, once forged in conflict's core,
Now seek repose on unfamiliar ground.

The walls, adorned with shadows of the night,
Hold whispered tales of battles long and past.
Yet in this space, beneath the dimmest light,
He finds a fleeting solace, brief but vast.

The cot he claims, a refuge from the fray,
Where dreams of home and hearth might intertwine.
Yet even here, the duty's constant sway,
Reminds his heart of honor's steep incline.

In every breath, he feels the world's embrace,
A soldier bound, yet yearning for his place.

A Soldier's Love, Unyielding Through the Fight

Amidst the clash of arms, his heart does yearn,
For tender moments with his distant love,
In every breath, her memory does burn,
A guiding star in darkened skies above.

Her image lingers in his weary mind,
A beacon bright, where shadows oft intrude,
Though war surrounds, her voice is soft and kind,
A melody that soothes his solitude.

He holds her letters close, their words so dear,
Each line a lifeline in the midst of war,
Her love, a shield against the creeping fear,
A promise that he'll soon return once more.

Though battle rages, love remains his guide,
A soldier's heart, with her, will e'er abide.

A Soldier's Parting

With heavy heart, he bids his bride adieu,
Her tear-streaked visage etched in memory's light,
As duty's call, unwavering and true,
Compels him forth into the shadowed night.

Their vows, so recently exchanged with grace,
Now tempered by the weight of fate's decree,
Her tender hand he clasps, a last embrace,
Before he journeys to the storm-tossed sea.

The silence lingers, filled with words unspoke,
Yet in their eyes, the truth of love remains,
Though miles shall stretch, and hearts by distance broke,
Their bond endures through duty's bitter strains.

For honor's sake, he leaves his love behind,
A soldier bound by duty, yet confined.

A Soldier's Repast:
The Quiet Hour of Peace

Amidst the chaos of the day's harsh fray,
The soldier finds a moment's brief repose,
Where rations simple on the tin plate lay,
A humble feast in midst of war's dark throes.

His weary hands, with strength not yet resigned,
Unclasp the fare that keeps his spirit whole,
In each small bite, a solace he doth find,
A respite for the body and the soul.

The murmurs of the camp, a distant hum,
While in this space, the world for once stands still,
His mind doth wander where no dangers come,
To homes afar and dreams he'll soon fulfill.

Yet as he eats, his thoughts must not delay,
For soon the call to arms will break this day.

A Soldier's Repose

Beneath the velvet shroud of starry night,
A soldier seeks the balm of fleeting rest,
His weary limbs, from battles fierce and bright,
Now crave the solace of the earth's cool breast.

The echoes of the day still haunt his mind,
In dreams where duty's call is never far,
Yet in this dark, a peace he hopes to find,
A brief reprieve beneath the watchful star.

The distant hum of war's relentless din,
Now fades into the silence of the skies,
While sleep, like velvet, gently folds him in,
And bids his troubled spirit close its eyes.

Yet even in this rest, he doth prepare,
For dawn's harsh light and war's unyielding glare.

A Soldier's Reprieve:
The Midday Meal Unshared

Amidst the clash of war, a fleeting pause,
Where comrades gather 'neath the fleeting sun,
In humble fare, they find a common cause,
A brief respite before the battle's run.

Their rations sparse, yet shared with quiet grace,
Each morsel savored with unspoken cheer,
In simple acts, their camaraderie's trace,
Evident in each bite and guarded leer.

The tin cups clink, a momentary peace,
In fields where strife and tumult oft convene,
A soldier's meal, where all hostilities cease,
In fleeting minutes, war's harshness turned serene.

Together they partake, yet minds afar,
On fields where soon they'll fight beneath the star.

Sanjay Kumar

A Soldier's Reverie in Twilight's Gloom

In martial fields, where strife and chaos reign,
A soldier broods on life once soft and mild,
Where tranquil days in bucolic domain
Withdrew the tumult, and his heart beguiled.

He recollects the sylvan, verdant glade,
Where zephyrs whispered through the ancient trees,
The placid brook where languid hours played,
And time meandered with unhurried ease.

Yet now, encased in armor's cold embrace,
He battles specters in the moonless night,
While visions of his past in dreams retrace
The vestiges of peace, now out of sight.

In recollections, solace he doth find,
A soldier's soul to simpler days inclined.

A Soldier's Vigil: The Desert's Harsh Embrace

In barren wastes where scorching sun prevails,
The soldier treads on sands of burning gold,
Each step a trial, as the harsh wind wails,
A searing breath upon the desert cold.

The endless dunes, like waves, do rise and fall,
A ceaseless sea where shadows seldom lie,
Yet in this vast, desolate, sun-scorched sprawl,
His duty calls beneath the glaring sky.

No verdant shade to offer cool respite,
No gentle breeze to ease the burning day,
Yet steadfast still, he guards through endless night,
Where stars alone might light his weary way.

In desert's grasp, his spirit stands unbowed,
A soldier firm, beneath a sky uncowed.

Sanjay Kumar

A Soldier's Watch

Amidst the heights where eagles dare to soar,
The soldier climbs, with steadfast heart and will,
Each step a challenge on the craggy floor,
Where nature's might and man's resolve stand still.

The biting winds assail his weathered face,
As frosty peaks enshroud the world below,
Yet duty's call commands his every pace,
Through icy mists and fields of bitter snow.

Above the clouds, where silence holds its sway,
He guards the pass, a sentinel on high,
Unyielding as the ancient rocks that stay,
Though storms may rage and stars desert the sky.

In lofty realms, his vigil knows no end,
A soldier true, where earth and heaven blend.

A Soldier's Dream of Days Once Lived

Amidst the clash of arms and war's cruel din,
A soldier dreams of days in peaceful lands,
When life was soft, where love and joy had been,
And all was held within his gentle hands.

He sees the fields where golden sunlight lay,
The quiet streets where children laughed and played,
The humble home where he would end each day,
In calm embrace, where gentle words were said.

But now, the world is sharp with steel and fire,
The echoes of his past a distant song,
Yet in his heart, a deep and strong desire,
To walk again where he has yearned so long.

In dreams he lives the life he left behind,
A soldier's heart with peace is intertwined.

A Soldier's Nationalism

A patriot's heart, with fervor deeply stirred,
For his homeland, a sacred, hallowed ground.
His eyes, ablaze, with passion, courage spurred,
As duty calls, and honor can be found.

He marches on, a sentinel of might,
A defender of the realm, a noble quest.
His spirit soars, a beacon burning bright,
As he defends the land he loves the best.

A soldier's nationalism, a fervent flame,
That burns within, a steadfast, loyal heart.
He stands for freedom, honor, and good name,
A patriot's soul, forever torn apart.

A soldier's love, a testament to grace,
A bond that time and distance cannot erase.

A Village Heart Entwined

In distant fields where battles rage and roar,
He marches on, his heart a captive still,
For in the quiet village he adores,
She waits, her love untouched by war's cruel will.

Her days are long, with tender hopes that wane,
As memories of whispered vows grow faint,
Yet in her breast, undying, love remains,
A beacon bright against the world's complaint.

The village hums with life, but she's apart,
Her thoughts consumed by him who fights afar,
Each evening brings a pang within her heart,
As she beseeches heaven's distant star.

Though miles divide, their souls remain as one,
Till war's dark night gives way to love's bright sun

Beneath the Tempest's Reign

Beneath the storm's relentless, weeping skies,
The soldier treads, encased in sodden gear,
Each drop a shard that from the heavens flies,
Yet on he moves, undaunted by the drear.

The earth beneath his boots, a mire of clay,
Yields grudgingly to every weary stride,
While thunder's roar and lightning's fleeting play
Compose the hymn to which his steps abide.

The rain cascades, a curtain cold and dense,
Obscuring all but duty's narrow path,
Yet in his heart, there burns a fierce defense,
A flame unquenched by nature's raging wrath.

In rain's embrace, he marches, iron-clad,
A soldier bold, through storm and tempest mad.

Beneath the Tricolor's Resplendent Light

Beneath the tricolor's resplendent hue,

A soldier stands, his visage stern yet proud,

With valour's crest and patriotism true,

His heart enshrined in stripes and stars endowed.

In azure, saffron, and the verdant green,

He finds a symbol of his sacred vow,

The flag, a testament to hopes unseen,

An emblem of the land he swears to plow.

His uniform, though worn and battle-torn,

Reflects the grandeur of the nation's pride,

While duty's weight upon his shoulders borne,

Guides him through tempests with undaunted stride.

The tricolour waves, a beacon for the brave,

He guards its honour from the dawn to grave.

Clash of Valor

Upon the field where steel and fire dance,
A soldier stands, his spirit forged in flame.
In every breath, the pulse of fierce advance,
He charges forth, to meet the foe's dark claim.

The clash of swords resounds like thunder's roar,
As blood and sweat commingle in the fray.
No fear can sway him from the task of war,
His heart is set, his honour to obey.

Through chaos and the din of mortal strife,
He wields his blade with skill and righteous might.
Each parry, thrust, a testament to life,
Against the shadowed forces of the night.

Though peril looms, his courage stands alight,
A soldier's soul, unyielding in the fight.

Comrades in Arms: A Soldier's Sacred Bond

In battle's throes, where fear and courage blend,
Two soldiers stand as brothers, side by side,
With every stride, their fates in tandem mend,
Through fields where death and valor oft collide.

Their words unspoken, yet their hearts entwined,
In trials faced, their spirits forge a shield,
A bond that neither time nor pain can bind,
Their camaraderie in the battlefield.

Through tempest's wrath and war's relentless might,
They march as one, their souls in union strong,
In darkest hours, they share a common light,
A kinship wrought in fire and endless song.

As comrades true, they face the final test,
In life or death, together they find rest.

Enshrined in Tricolor

Beneath the heavens' mournful, muted hue,
He lies, a warrior taken by the fray,
His duty done, his journey carried through,
In silence now, he greets eternal day.

The tricolor, a shroud of sacred pride,
Embraces him in hues of valor bright,
Saffron, white, and green, in solemn stride,
Reflect the spirit of his noble fight.

No drum nor bugle now disturbs his peace,
Yet in the folds of India's cherished flag,
His legacy, undying, shall increase,
A beacon where the brave dare not to lag.

Though death has stilled his heart, his honor stands,
Enwrapped in freedom's triune, loving hands.

Fallen Hero

A valiant soul, a warrior true and bold,
He fell in battle, on a foreign shore.
His life was sacrificed, a story untold,
A hero's tale, forevermore.

A noble heart, a spirit pure and bright,
He faced the foe with courage unsurpassed.
Though darkness claimed him in the midst of night,
His legacy shall never be surpassed.

His sacrifice, a beacon shining clear,
A testament to valor, love, and might.
Though tears may fall, and sorrow may appear,
His memory shall forever burn so bright.

So let us honor him, this fallen friend,
A hero's death, a life that will transcend.

Sanjay Kumar

Forge of Iron Will

Amidst the echo of the morning's call,
The soldier stands where discipline is wrought.
In structured ranks, they rise, both firm and tall,
Their every step with purpose deeply fraught.

The training ground, a crucible of might,
Where strength is honed and weakness cast aside.
Each challenge faced beneath the watchful sight,
Of those who shape the steel in which they bide.

Through arduous trials and sweat-stained days,
Their bodies bend, yet never do they break.
The forge of duty burns in countless ways,
As every soul is tempered for the stake.

Emerging from this crucible of fire,
A soldier stands, fulfilled in true desire.

In Distant Lands, My Heart Remains Behind

In distant lands, a soldier stands so tall,
With duty's weight upon his weary frame,
Yet thoughts of home do echo in the hall,
Where echoes whisper but a single name.

His son, a boy, who roams the village green,
Beneath the skies of innocence and grace,
With dreams untouched by war's relentless sheen,
And laughter brightening every humble space.

The soldier fights with courage in his heart,
But in his dreams, his son's small hand he holds,
Through every battle, though they are apart,
It is his boy's sweet face his mind unfolds.

Though far away, in fields of dust and strife,
His love remains, the beacon of his life.

On the Hallowed Heights

Amidst the peaks where heavens kiss the earth,
A soldier treads the paths where eagles soar.
Each step he takes, a testament of worth,
Through icy winds that bite and tempests roar.

The jagged cliffs, his steadfast battleground,
Where nature's wrath and man's resolve collide.
No soft reprieve, no gentle, fertile ground,
But rugged stone where fortitude is tried.

In solitude, beneath the starry sprawl,
He guards the realm where silence reigns supreme.
Each breath a vow, each heartbeat duty's call,
In hallowed heights where dreams and valor teem.

The mountains echo with his solemn tread,
A soldier's watch, where fear and doubt have fled.

Parting from His Hearth

Upon the threshold of his distant fate,
The soldier turns, his heart a heavy stone,
With every step, he leaves behind the gate
Of home, where love and solace once were known.

The hearth's warm glow now fades from sight and mind,
As duty's call compels his steadfast stride,
Yet in his thoughts, the memories entwined
Of whispered farewells and a tearful bride.

The fields he once did till with tender care,
Now lie in wait, untended and forlorn,
While he, through war's bleak landscape, must repair,
Bereft of all for which his soul was born.

In lands afar, his spirit shall remain,
A soldier bound by love, yet torn by pain.

Sanjay Kumar

Sentinel of the Line

Beneath the watchful sky, on rugged ground,
A soldier stands where lands in tension meet.
The border's breath, a whispered, restless sound,
Commands his vigilance, denies retreat.

The cold winds cut, like blades through armor's shield,
Yet still he holds his post with iron will.
Each footfall on the barren, frozen field,
Echoes the oath that binds him silent, still.

Beyond the wire, a world in shadows lurks,
Unknown, unseen, yet always felt so near.
In every breath, the weight of duty works,
To quell the rising tide of doubt and fear.

Though miles from home, he guards the fragile line,
A sentinel where day and night entwine.

Soldier's Departure

A heavy heart, a tearful, sad adieu,
As duty calls, and he must march away.
A final kiss, a promise to be true,
To fight with valor, come what may.

The train departs, a mournful, distant sound,
As loved ones watch, their hearts with sorrow filled.
The soldier's gaze, upon the ground,
His spirit heavy, his resolve unkilled.

A noble cause, a duty to fulfill,
 A sacrifice he willingly will make.
Though fears may linger, his heart is still,
A steadfast soul, for freedom's sake.

So let him go, with courage and with pride,
 A hero's journey, where he'll bravely ride.

Sanjay Kumar

Soldier's Farewell

Adieu, my love, my heart's most precious part,
Whose tender gaze can soothe my troubled soul.
Though duty calls, and I must now depart,
Your love shall guide me, steadfast and whole.

The battlefield awaits, a hostile land,
 Where danger lurks and courage must prevail.
Yet, in your love, I'll find a guiding hand,
 A beacon bright that shall forever hail.

So fare thee well, my dearest, sweetest wife,
 Until the day when I return to thee.
 May peace and joy fill every moment of your life,
And may your love forever be my guide.

Though duty calls, my heart will ever stay,
With you, my love, come what may.

Soldier's Quarters

Within the billet's walls, a weary soul,
A soldier's respite from the battlefield.
A humble dwelling, where the shadows prowl,
And echoes whisper tales of woe and yield.

A simple room, where memories reside,
Of battles fought, of comrades lost to war.
A place of solace, where he can abide,
And find a moment's peace, though scarred and sore.

The creaking floorboards, a familiar sound,
The musty air, a heavy, stifling weight.
Yet, in this space, a sanctuary is found,
A refuge from the chaos, the relentless fate.

So let him rest, this weary soldier's frame,
Within the billet's walls, his humble claim.

Sanjay Kumar

Soldier's Slumber

Beneath a canvas canopy, he lies,
A weary warrior, worn by endless strife.
The moonlit sky, a silent, starlit prize,
A fleeting glimpse of peace in mortal life.

A restless sleep, disturbed by phantom fears,
Of battle's rage and comrades lost to war.
His mind is haunted by the haunting years,
The scars of conflict, etched upon his core.

Yet, in his dreams, he finds a fleeting peace,
A glimpse of home, of loved ones far away.
A respite from the turmoil, a sweet release,
A moment's solace in the darkest day.

So let him sleep, this weary soldier's soul,
And may his dreams bring comfort and console.

Soldier's Summit

A sentinel of stone, a steadfast guard,
 He stands upon the mountain's rugged crest,
Where winds of winter howl, a tempest's bard,
And icy fingers pierce his armored chest.

The peaks, his fortress, towering o'er the land,
 A silent vigil, under starlit sky.
The valleys stretch, a vast, untamed expanse,
 Where shadows creep and dangers multiply.

With eagle's eye, he scans the distant plain,
For any sign of threat, a lurking foe.
His heart, a beacon, burning bright and plain,
A steadfast spirit, resolute and slow.

A solitary post, a lonely plight,
Yet duty calls, and he will stand and fight.

Soldier's Sustenance

A meager meal, a respite from the fray,
A moment's peace amidst the chaos' roar.
With weary hands, he clumsily conveys
The rations issued, day by day.

A tinned delight, a tasteless, bland affair,
A stark reminder of the war's grim plight.
Yet, as he eats, he whispers silent prayer,
For strength and courage to endure the night.

A soldier's fare, a simple, humble feast,
A sustenance that fuels his weary frame.
Though far from home, his spirit is released,
As he reflects upon his noble aim.

For in this meal, a purpose he discerns,
A duty owed, a flame that brightly burns.

Solitary Soldier

In tattered uniform, he stands alone,
A weary soul, adrift in war's harsh tide.
His eyes, once bright, now clouded, fear unknown,
 As death's cold hand draws ever closer, wide.

Destitute and lost, a fragile shell,
He seeks a haven, where he can find peace.
A life once filled with hope, now shattered spell,
As sorrows deep within his soul increase.

His comrades fallen, his spirit crushed,
A soldier's heart, forever scarred by pain.
 In war's cold grip, his dreams are utterly hushed,
As solitude's dark shadow does remain.

A solitary soul, far from home, he roams,
A victim of war, where sorrow blooms.

Sanjay Kumar

The Fallen Warrior

Upon the field where valor meets its fate,
He falls, a hero in the crimson dust,
His sacrifice, the toll of duty's weight,
In silent honor, all his comrades trust.

The echo of his life now softly fades,
Yet in the hearts he leaves, his spirit shines,
A beacon in the dark, through war's cruel shade,
His courage carved in time's enduring lines.

No more the battle's roar shall he attend,
Nor see the dawn that breaks o'er peaceful lands,
Yet in the whispers of the wind, his friend,
His legacy remains in sacred hands.

Though death has claimed his mortal form to sleep,
His memory the living vow to keep.

The Half-Belly's Lament

With hunger gnawing deep, a silent fiend,
The soldier marches on, resolve held tight,
His meager rations, scarcely to be gleaned,
Yet fortitude sustains him through the night.

A crust of bread, a sip of water's grace,
The scanty fare that barely fuels his might,
But in his heart, no weakness finds a place,
For duty's call transcends his appetite.

The growl within, a beast that won't relent,
Yet still he stands, unbowed by want or woe,
In every stride, his will and strength are bent,
Against the pangs that lesser men might know.

Though belly starved, his spirit knows no dearth,
A soldier's pride outweighs his hunger's worth.

Sanjay Kumar

The Snowy Evening's Gaze

Upon the frozen earth where silence reigns,
The soldier stands, enshrouded in the white,
The snowfall drapes the land in crystal chains,
A frigid cloak that veils the coming night.

Each breath he draws is met with winter's sting,
A biting chill that gnaws at flesh and bone,
Yet in his heart, a steadfast flame does cling,
A warmth that neither ice nor cold has known.

The quiet hush of snow's descent doth fill
The air with whispers, soft as angel's breath,
And though the night grows darker, colder still,
He holds his post, defying winter's death.

In this bleak hour, amidst the frost and freeze,
The soldier stands, a sentinel with ease.

The Soldier Grandma, Brave in Heart and Deed

With gentle hands, she holds her grandchild near,
A soldier's heart within her beats so strong,
Her tales of courage bring both awe and cheer,
As she recounts the battles fought so long.

In every wrinkle lies a story told,
Of nights on watch beneath a starlit sky,
Her spirit, forged in days both harsh and bold,
Yet softened now by love's enduring tie.

She once wore boots that marched through mud and rain,
With steadfast steps that never feared the fight,
But now she treads a path of lesser pain,
Her battlefield replaced by warmth and light.

A soldier grandma, valor in her veins,
Her legacy of love and strength remains.

The Soldier Grandma, with Valor and Grace

Beneath the twilight's calm, her visage glows,
A soldier once, now matron of the clan,
In history's annals, her boldness shows,
A valor rare in every seasoned span.

Her voice recounts the epic, storied days,
Where courage met the fiercest foe's advance,
Her deeds etched deep in time's unyielding ways,
Yet tempered now by time's soft, tender dance.

The medals worn, though tarnished, still confer,
A testament to battles bravely fought,
Her legacy, a beacon that shall blur
The lines of peace and war with lessons taught.

A soldier grandma, in her sagely grace,
Preserves the wars within her gentle face.

The Soldier Grandpa, With Stories to Impart

He sits beneath the oak, in twilight's glow,
A soldier once, now grandpa to the young,
His tales of valor, battles long ago,
Are spoken softly in his weathered tongue.

The medals on his chest, a silent pride,
Yet in his eyes, the echoes of the past,
With every story told, the tears subside,
As laughter brightens memories so vast.

The children gather 'round his rocking chair,
Their eyes wide open, listening with delight,
For though the years have silvered all his hair,
His heart remains as strong as in the fight.

In every word, a life of courage gleams,
A soldier grandpa, living in his dreams.

Sanjay Kumar

The Soldier's Bride, Awaiting His Return

She waits alone, the soldier's bride so true,
Her heart entwined with his in distant lands,
Through every night, the war's cold winds she knew,
Yet dreams of him still warm her gentle hands.

The gown she wears is white as morning light,
A symbol of the love they vowed to keep,
Though war has torn him from her tender sight,
Her faith in him runs steadfast, strong, and deep.

Each letter from the front she holds with care,
A treasure of the words he bravely writes,
In every line, his love she finds laid bare,
A beacon bright through war's relentless nights.

She knows that one day he will come again,
Her soldier's love, her joy, her truest friend.

The Soldier's Dedication to the Realm

In valor's name, he pledges unfeigned fealty,
A soldier sworn to guardianship of land,
His duty etched in realms of loyalty,
With steadfast heart and disciplined command.

Upon the morrow's brink, his vigil holds,
Against the tempest's wrath and darkest bane,
His ardor for the realm in silence molds,
To stave off shadows with unyielding strain.

Through strife and tumult, where the war cries soar,
His resolve stands as citadel and shield,
A paragon of valor evermore,
Defending freedom's rights upon the field.

His dedication, pure as driven snow,
A soldier's oath in service does bestow.

Sanjay Kumar

The Soldier's Duty
to the Sovereign State

In martial guise, the soldier swears his oath,
To safeguard realms with vigilance unbowed,
His duty fixed, a beacon to the troth,
Where honour's call through tumult does resound.

His limbs endure the rigours of the fray,
Beneath the banner of the sovereign might,
Through tempests fierce and on the brink of day,
He stands, a bulwark 'gainst the encroaching night.

With every stride, the weight of duty bears,
A consecration to the land he guards,
His sacrifice, though hidden from the lairs,
Defends the peace from darkened, vengeful shards.

In dedication, his heart finds its grace,
A soldier's pledge, for freedom's steadfast place.

The Soldier's Duty

With iron will, the soldier stands aligned,
His oath to serve, a sacred, solemn vow,
In every deed, his heart and soul combined,
To duty's cause, he bends both time and brow.

No task too great, no peril he shall shun,
For in his breast, a fire eternal burns,
Each battle fought, each victory hard-won,
To honor's call, his steadfast soul returns.

Through storm and strife, his path remains unswayed,
A beacon bright amidst the darkest night,
By honor's light and loyalty arrayed,
He marches on, with courage as his might.

In duty's name, he treads where few would dare,
A soldier true, with burdened heart laid bare.

The Soldier's Fall: A Sacrifice in Strife

Beneath the crimson sky, where battle raged,
A soldier stood, his heart both fierce and true,
In war's embrace, where destinies are waged,
He fought with valor that but few men knew.

With every clash, his spirit undeterred,
Against the tide of foes that pressed him near,
Yet fate, in shadows, whispered her last word,
And stilled his breath, despite his lack of fear.

He fell, a hero in the throes of war,
His lifeblood mingling with the soil he saved,
The battlefield his final, fateful shore,
Where courage met the silence of the grave.

His name, enshrined in honor's sacred tome,
A soldier's death, his sacrifice our home.

The Soldier's Nationalist Embrace

With fervent heart, he dons the battle's guise,
A soldier staunch, enshrined in valor's creed,
His gaze imbued with fervid, patriotic eyes,
To serve his land with unrelenting speed.

Upon the field, where liberty's bright flame
Burns through the darkened veils of foreign night,
He stands, a sentinel with honor's name,
Defending realms with undying might.

In every clash, his spirit's zealous thrall,
Proclaims allegiance to the sacred soil,
Where freedoms reign and shadows dare not sprawl,
He strives, through blood and sweat, to guard and toil.

Nationalism's fire in his veins does surge,
A soldier's sacrifice, in dreams and urge.